Ins and Outs

Poems and Stories from the 70's

By

Suzanne Brooks

The stories in this book are works of fiction. Places, events, and situations in them are purely fictional. Any resemblance in these stories to actual persons, living or dead, is coincidental.

ISBN: 1-4140-1757-X (e-book)
ISBN: 1-4140-2968-3 (Paperback)

Library of Congress Control Number: 2003097911

This book is printed on acid free paper.

Printed in the United States of America
Bloomington, IN

1stBooks – rev. 12/01/03

Dedicated
To
The One I love

Suzanne Brooks, vocalist, hula dancer, community activist, educator and entrepreneur, since 1979, has worked as Multi-Cultural Center Director, California State University, Sacramento; Affirmative Action Officer, Penn State University; Science Supportive Services Director, Washington State University; and at Heald College of Business. She is currently completing her EdD in Educational Leadership and Change at the Fielding Institute—dissertation, "Racism and Sexism in Higher Education:the Autoethnography of an Activist."

Ms. Brooks owns two businesses: Creative Concepts Systems, a business consulting firm, and *the International Association for Women of Color Day*.

Ms. Brooks studies Speech-Level Singing (SLS) at Seth Riggs vocal camps, in LA and with SLS Coach, Reinhardt Krekow. She has had vocal coaching from Chris Beatty of Nashville, TN and Lucy McKinney, Sacramento. She studies piano with jazz pianist and gospel music director, Reggie Graham. She is currently performing and recording two CDs—collections of jazz standards with Eric Tillman (previously with the Temptations, Impressions, Willie Bobo and numerous jazz venues.) Tillman is her music director/accompanist/arranger.

Ms. Brooks co-authored and performed the choreopoem, "The Strength of Sisterly Love" at the 2002 Harlem Theatre Fringe Festival. Also in 2002 at Sacramento's Interactive Asian Contemporary Theatre, she played "Tutu" in the World Premiere of "The Canoe." She also sang new and traditional songs in Hawaiian language, later recording "Angel's Blues" with it's composer, pianist and slack key guitarist, George Winston. Recently, she appeared in a 10-week run of "The King and I" at Garbeau's Dinner Theatre, Sacramento. She has danced with the Hapa Haole Hula Dancers for more than eight years.

Ms. Brooks is a board member of Women-and-Life-on-Earth (international women's peace organization), president of the Jack Hall Foundation (for unwed mothers), and president of California Sol, a women of color/cultural research institute.

TABLE OF CONTENTS

Biographical Note from 1979 Edition
(Published in India)

Suzanne Pope Brooks resides in Pullman, Washington, USA, where she has just completed work for a master's degree in English/Creative Writing at Washington State University. In 1975, she received a B.A. in English and Education from LaSalle College, Philadelphia, PA. In the same year, she was awarded a Danforth Fellowship and published her first short story, "Light Through The Ivy" in *Essence Magazine*.

Ms. Brooks has worked as an editor for a variety of publications, including literary magazines at LaSalle College and Washington State University. She has given readings of her poems (on occasion in simultaneous sign language) in Alabama, Pennsylvania and Washington. From 1965 to 1972, Ms. Brooks worked as a Philadelphia Police Officer. In 1968, she was a co-founder of Girls, Inc., a non-profit organization for inner-city Philadelphia girls. Ms. Brooks is guardian of two children, Paul and Daryl, who live with her in Pullman. The poems in this collection were composed between 1973 and 1978.

INTRODUCTION

For the black, female writer in 1977, coming to terms with the intent and function of the craft is no simple task. Unless she keeps her work private, there is a danger of pejorative critical labeling as a "black writer" or "woman writer," suggesting a limited view or narrow audience. Yet no one writes without an experiential base and for the black woman writer, the characteristic aspects of her being, the roots of her experiences, are those aspects most likely to be pointed out as indicators of her limits. Such opinions should not persist and, indeed, if an assessment of the many influences upon my work is made, it will be evident that the black, female writer is not inherently limited but subject to the ordinary limitations of educational level, experience, and exposure to other artists and art forms which confront all writers. The comments which follow are aimed at offering insights into the accompanying poems and stories. One fact is central—my self-conception is that of being black, a woman, and a writer, simultaneously, with no ordering of priority. The order in which these concerns are discussed is purely an arbitrary one.

Many black writers have preceded me in addressing the general problems facing blacks in America. Langston Hughes, at times biting, rarely bitter, conveys a sense of hopefulness even in moments of deep despair. The hope is made possible, at times, through the use of ironic humor in poems like "Life is Fine."

Though you may hear me holler,
And you may see me cry—
I'll be dogged, sweet baby,
If you gonna see me die.

I have striven to echo that combination of affrontery, hope, despair, and humor in "Ins and Outs." Of additional significance to me is the fact that "Ins and Outs" was the result of my first concerted effort to give vent to my own black, inner-city voice. The attention which Langston Hughes gives to the anguish experienced by persons of interracial heritage has drawn me repeatedly to explorations of the same theme. In "Cross," Hughes ponders the future of a half-black, half-white child who has repudiated both worlds. In "Achromatic Matter," I am concerned with the rejection of interracial offspring by those they love. The theme is repeated in my short story, "Light Through the Ivy."

Imamu Amiri Baraka, in the change of his name from LeRoi Jones, symbolizes, for me, the repudiation of a value system designed to repress whole peoples. His rejection has arisen with the development of a justified anger and healthy aggressiveness which point the way to survival for other black writers. In "Paraleipsis," my aim is to strengthen Baraka's argument by assisting in the formation of new values by pointing out previously unrecognized heroes. "On the Death of Elijah Muhammad" represents an admission of past failure to recognize the pioneers of a new black consciousness, which is inherently political. Thus, Baraka's involvement in the politics of Newark, New Jersey seems, to me, the logical extension of his poems and a precedent I follow in utilizing my own as vehicles for social change. Because of my experiences with many hearing-impaired friends and relatives, my efforts are directed toward change, not only for blacks and other people of color, but also for the handicapped. For me, then, my poem "Handicapped," and my uses of sign language are, in part, the consequence of arguments begun by Baraka.

Several black women have been important to my development as a writer. Gwendolyn Brooks has been influential only to the extent that, with few exceptions, her formality of style has been that which I avoid emulating. In contrast, Maya Angelou's novel, *I Know Why the Caged Bird Sings* (1970), and collection of poems, *Just Give Me a Cool Drink of Water 'fore I Diiie* (1971), have sparked my imagination to find avenues for the expression of small moments of personal emotion which can be captured in a few words—in the spirit, if not the form, of haiku. Angelou's rhythmic sense, demonstrated in "Times-Square-Shoeshine-Composition," is a direct influence in my experiments coupling drums or music with my poems.

Lucille Clifton, who is close to my own age and a lover and mother of many children, is of more importance to me as a model than any other writer. Better known to many as a writer of children's stories, Clifton has produced three small books of poetry in which she examines her domestic life, her heritage and herself. In her third book of poems, *An Ordinary Woman* (1974), Clifton addresses a wide variety of issues—from fighting roaches to coming to terms with the ordinariness of her life. She has served me more than once as an example of a poet who is personal without resorting to confession, attentive to small details without becoming trite. I have been guided by the lines of Clifton's poems in portraying relationships with my own children in "Adoption After-piece" and "Current Events," both of which concern brief moments or incidents of lasting significance.

It would be inaccurate to suggest that I have not been influenced by the changing roles for women—modifications which have been substantial in my lifetime—but despite my affinity for "feminist" writers such as Erica Jong, I no longer identify altogether with what is commonly referred to as the women's liberation movement. My perception at this time is that the women's movement is a vehicle for changes which can only minimally affect my situation as long as the society-at-large remains essentially racist. Nevertheless, a profound influence for me has been the work of Anne Sexton. The impact of Sexton's poetry was greatly enhanced by my meeting her, a few months before her death. That meeting unmasked the extreme isolation engulfing some writers and warned me of the dangers of confessionalism. As a consequence, I strive for the personal element, but avoid the confession, preferring to utilize a persona always. This practice is an inviolable rule for both my poetry and prose.

The poetry of John Berryman is a major influence upon my own work; his dream songs demonstrate the potential of the subconscious in the creation of art. Some of the poems included in this collection are the result of efforts to capture dreams. Several lines of "An Odyssean Dream" originated in a dream. In addition to the stress on dreams, I concur with Berryman on the importance of the autobiographical element within a work. Though I believe that it is not necessary that autobiography be immediately apparent to the reader, I am convinced that the personality of the writer as shaped by environment is the primary determinant of content.

The function of my writing varies with the form. That is, the form is suited to the function intended. In poetry, my effort is directed toward the writing of those essential words which, when coupled with a reading performance, will engulf the audience in the sense and emotion of the writer at the moment of creation. Frequently, such moments are the reactions to social stress, which accounts for their effectiveness in performance—the audience and the poet constituting a social setting. The poems are completed in the exchange which occurs. Most of my poetry is intended to function as dramatic script for performance. Following the rationale of earlier writers of oratory, several poems have been presented as segments of oratorical addresses. In performance, the overall movement is toward a revolutionary consciousness which aims to bring about political change. In efforts to increase audience sense of involvement, I make use of musical or drum accompaniment and simultaneous manual sign language. On occasion, sections of a poem may be sung or chanted. Attention is also given to props and costuming wherever possible. All special effects are suited to the message intended and the audience expected to receive it. Though concentrating on my own work, performances often include the work of other writers to demonstrate the fusion of the universal among writers.

The function of my fiction differs from that of the poetry in that it is the result of a more extended and sustained state of mind and does not require any accompanying physical activity by the writer. The combination of narrative and dialogue permits the social exchange to take place within the work—an exchange not usually achievable within the brief space of a poem.

Because fiction is not performable, it cannot be aided by personality directly or by other external activities and is dependent solely upon the reader's response to the printed page. The subjects of my fiction are drawn from life—generally the lives of others, but often from some personal experience of my own which brings the outside nearer and in sharper than usual focus. It is rarely possible for me to make use of recent experiences. Rather I keep notes that become usable only after the passage of extended periods of time. The fact that I have done a substantial amount of journalistic writing, and continue to do so, has resulted in my habit of writing about recent events in a style more appropriate to a news report than to a short story. This does not appear to be a disability for me, but gives me yet another vehicle for expression. Upon completion of the first draft of a short story, I usually find it necessary to revise extensively to achieve greater differentiation of character voices. Often, during revision, I shift the narrator's point of view. Alterations of grammar, punctuation, names and titles, I leave until last.

No introduction to this collection would be complete without the mention of two professors who taught me during my undergraduate years at LaSalle College. Professor Richard Lautz, who encouraged and provided opportunities for readings of my poems in workshops around the city of Philadelphia, is responsible for the development of my interest in poetry as a performing art. Professor Claude Koch taught me the rigors of the craft and the value of tough and honest criticism. Above all, I am haunted by his single most repeated word—"revise." More importantly, Mr. Koch led me to accept the loneliness of the craft and the necessity of patience and humility. It is particularly meaningful that my first published short story was written for his creative writing workshop.

Prefatory Note to Poems

Most of the poems in this collection are intended to be read aloud. Although this does not preclude a silent reading, it will be helpful to the reader to keep the intended performance in mind. In an effort to assist the reader in visualizing the intended effect, the following notes to key poems are provided.

"Ins and Outs" is a poem I read most often to gatherings of women, black people, or those considering themselves sophisticated and liberal. The stance taken by the persona (I define it this way because I consider myself to be acting a role) is that of a street-wise, fast-talking city woman whose slight Southern drawl is a clue to a softer, more sensitive women trying to come to terms with changing norms and unchanging attitudes. The first seven lines are delivered in a deliberately sensual tone accompanied by slightly provocative body movements. With the eighth line, the tone is shifted to one of thoughtfulness and confidentiality. Thereafter the poem alternates between moods of sensuality and anger at insensitiveness, free expression of emotion and hidden feelings under bitter retorts. The poem is most effectively delivered when carried out as if in intimate conversation with a member of the audience. The rest of the audience then responds as if eavesdropping on an embarrassing conversation.

"Positions" is a good lead-in for remarks and later discussions of racism in America. The aim of the persona is to convince the audience that she is an authority of sorts on the subject. This is accompanied by an open, forthright manner which deteriorates into a seemingly blind, pleading naiveté which ends the first stanza. The second stanza opens with the same pleading tone, drawn to the level of the ridiculous until the middle of the fourth line and the word "hate" which unmasks the persona and the threat of aggression in the balance of the poem.

Most audiences like to think that some secret knowledge of the poet will be gained during the reading. "Electricity" is a poem which plays on this desire. Few bits of information are more quickly devoured than insights into an erotic nature. Thus, the delivery of "Electricity" requires the confiding tone and manner of a confession of great guilt for the first stanza. The second stanza is delivered as if by a bemused wanton, a tone maintained for the first seven lines of the third stanza. Thereafter, the persona shifts to a tone of tenderness which diminishes into a childlike, almost child-sounding voice of innocence. "Electricity" is further enhanced by the simultaneous use of manual sign language. The repeated references to the senses and sensual are easier images to portray with sign language than more abstract or philosophical poems would be.

THE POEMS

Suzanne Brooks

INFLUENCES

Mine was the beat generation
long before the fifties.
I was born in the year
of Pearl Harbor.
My parents were patriots.

Daddy went to France:
A segregated soldier sent
against Nazis, he left
my bastard brother there,
Brought home a taste for wine.

Mother aided the war work,
welding ships to bring the boys
home. Women like her kept up
morale by aborting the babies
other soldiers left behind.

Everywhere, there was a joint
effort. Everybody got screwed.

When I write my autobiography,
there will be at least one
chapter on bombs, how they have
shaped my life by falling on
others who weren't white either.

The age of –ins aimed at
making changes is past.
Left is a mass of memories
haunted by a lack of diversity.
Everywhere, I am still Black.

Like my father, I fight
a war begun by someone else.

Here, across the continent
from my origins, I seek
another beginning amidst
a people more barren
than the city's concrete.

Perhaps it is the arid inland
and the absence of trees
that makes these people
so much like those I
have sought to escape.

Perhaps in the evolution
of things, humanity has
become too rooted in dirt.

Suzanne Brooks

CLASS LINES

They sit encircled
whispering words
of wisdom reamed
from books and
dreamed from drugs
like so many
bugs relishing what
is only garbage.
They wear denim
badges and love
that fades in
the sober morning.
They rap with
the blackest in
any place long
as their liberal
point can be
seen. But we
would rather deal
with roaches. They're
a lot easier to
kill.

ON THE DEATH OF ELIJAH MUHAMMAD

Your live words
made the white cringe
in me. I forded you
cleverly and with jeers.
Your leaving
leaves no vacuum,
no tears, only
a surfeited pride
flooding from some dark
part of me which
must have loved you,
though I never knew.

Suzanne Brooks

POSITIONS

Where I'm at is constantly
changing. I remember
sitting in the front
of a church that was
all white the day after
being on the side
of the movie where
the faces were all Black.

I didn't see any
discrimination in that.
I thought I was just
sitting with my friends.

I have always tried being
rational when it comes
to religion. I love
the music and hate
the ritual of every
faith I know, 'cause
none of 'em takes a stand
for what I am.

THE SNAKE BASKET

The snake basket hangs
In the window, filled
With a creeping vine.
It is a symbol
Of all my fears.

The snake basket came
From the east, a gift
From a friend. It is
Only to friends that
I am vulnerable.

The snake basket lid
Is open. Soon, ivy will
Cover it over. It is
Always what is most
Familiar that is most insidious.

Suzanne Brooks

SUMMARY

A few blond strands
Mixed with fewer gray
Give sheen to the solemn
Brown hair hanging long
Over slightly plump shoulders.
From behind, the jeaned,
Sweatered roundness seems
Of a budding virgin.
Once merry brows frame
Cat-green, cat-alert eyes
That catch even the smallest
Movement or slightest detail.
Edging crow's feet expose
At close range that youth
Here is merely mirage.
Unaffected by fashion,
She will be remembered
In blue bandanas, accepted
More than understood. When
Her one child grows up
And away to some renown,
Few will remember this
Mother; none will know
Her. Still, she will go on
Searching among the world's
Litter, open to the small
Needs that she can fill.

BRIDGE #1

I stare
through my window
at a browning hill
and men, who
since first light
have been building
a house.
This new world
looms under clouds
that do not dim
the light.
I wait for
last remnants
of another life
now destroyed by fire
and with them
all those bridges
to my past.

Suzanne Brooks

TEDIUM

There is no agony
greater than the mind
straining to alertness
when the body craves sleep.
The haze of a cloud,
hung before eyes, makes
clear the distances between
things; and it is not always
possible to move closer or shut eyes.

MOTHER

The fight, if there was one,
Is over.
Perhaps there is a God
And church is not just
A waste of time
Still, (thank God) we are different
If I sing my sons
The songs of my childhood,
It is that I never learned others;
Not that I want to recall
Your soft, purring voice.
Yes, education is important,
But that idea is not yours alone.
If I agree, it is not with you.
(If you can understand that,
why did you never understand me?
If you are my enemy,
Why do I need
To explain anything?
The answer is why I have
Given up the battle as lost.

Suzanne Brooks

CURRENT EVENTS

Fourteen, you walk
away in February
snow, last vestiges
of infancy falling
away like flakes.

You do not know
today's news is
centered on a Black
man's murdering
in Uganda.

The snow has not
yet melted into slush.

SPOKANE

Walkers of rain-soaked streets
stare at non-existent stars.
Sleepers beneath neon signs
keep muddied dreams.
Men whose beards drip spit
wait out the hours of oldness
like a job, while the working class
passes by this street scene
with a shudder, secure
that *they* were never begetters
of the rest of us.

Suzanne Brooks

FIRST WOMAN COALMINER

The beam from your helmet
undimmed by the dust,
you emerge from more
than a mine.
From my own dark hole
I look hard at you,
digging my own way out
into the light.

DOOR

When I am happy
You are open
And I touch you softly.

Frustrated,
I slam you
Into place.

In anger,
I pound you,
Almost tearing you apart.

But you are the stronger
Of us, unmoved
By anything I do.

Always standing ready
To serve me. Mute
Tool of my emotions.

Suzanne Brooks

PROGRESSION

The rain in all those want-filled days
of ragged clothes and roaches
washed away the dirt and cold
of being poor. We laughed and splashed
in storms now forgotten
in today's neat row house
with well-poured martini.
Yet, when I consider
The sterile, insulate future,
I stand in the sun alone,
on the verge of tears.

PARALEIPSIS
(for Doris Johnson and Doris Johnson)

Perhaps there is something
in the name Johnson
that speaks of slave
backgrounds in faces
of African women
who stand tall
among the rest
of us; a remnant
in the name Doris
of old 'ligioned
Mamas who named you
after dead sisters
or a saint. You
are so far apart
and alike as only
stark Black women
boosting children and men
can be. Some
share your pain:
the secret, silent
facing of so many
hopes crushed by
too much giving
too little left of self.
You bear other names.
You are more than two.

Suzanne Brooks

GNATS

No one alone could hurt
Beyond that momentary sting.
A single pair of wings
Utters no sound.
But swarming, your flight looms,
A roaring storm cloud
Intent on eroding away
The last of my flesh.

FOR ERICA JONG, WITH WARMEST WISHES

We could have eggs
in common, but you boil
I fry and eggs alone
are not enough.

My friends wonder why
you write of Africa.
I know nothing of that
place. Your friends
will be surprised.
Laugh with me.

How did you finish
the book I began
long before? It is
still beginning.

To answer your note
sent to unknown me
because I professed
admiration: Sister,
this adulation
springs from envy.

Suzanne Brooks

LIES

Smooth sees slide easily
Down my throat, against
My will; force me to anticipate
The inevitable strangulation.

Sleek words flatter
My defenseless vanity
Until I choke
On the truth.

BRIDGE #2

When you were five
and I twelve,
You hated my kissing
You at recess
but could not tell me.

We have never
talked about this
love between us
which has endured
others and ourselves.

So many women
bind themselves
to men with children.
Barren, I am no different.
My diluted blood flows
in your motherless child.

When you leave again
because I have
crowded you into
too small a corner,
You will go without warning.
You have not changed, Brother.

Suzanne Brooks

A QUESTION OF TASTE

Every day
live collage
welfare, clinics,
insults, fear;
and you
tell me if
I write about
it, I will
be out
of style
next year?

ANNE SEXTON (APRIL, 1974)

Christ-woman
Moving past me
Toward the stage,
Transformed in ascension
To immortal drama,
Your coat removed
Bares your stigmata
And all the multitude
Hover about,
Seeing you quiver,
Blind to your truth.
I could tell you
I understand,
But you don't know me.
In a minute
Your agony ends
As you descend again;
Or do you fall, Angel,
To hell with the rest of us?
A child at your feet,
I gaze up at you in sorrow
That you must die.

Note to the reader: Anne Sexton committed suicide in October, 1974, six months after this poem was written.

Suzanne Brooks

INSIGHT

One thing about God
he sure can pick 'em
(me being one of
the chosen few).

FOR TWO ANNES—SEXTON AND MAXWELL

Annie, No matter what
They do to me,
I will choose
My own downfall.

Suzanne Brooks

REBUFF

Your look
into my letters
tells me
not to die
because the note
I leave is not
suitable to the mood.

Not reading, you
say I tear myself
apart for nothing
and hand me a napkin
to wipe it all away.

You were
never me.
You cannot write
my epitaph.

AN ODYSSEAN DREAM
To Richard Lautz

Richard, you have engaged me
in a frightening love affair
that hounds me awake
though my body craves
sleep. I have dreamt
of tucking you in my bed.

You have become my nightmare
insatiably whipping away
the walls I have so carefully
constructed to hide myself
from myself and you.

I am standing before
the great poet and you
are urging with smiles
become sinister: "one more,
one more." You will
never be sated.
I try

To confess the flood
of feeling threatening
to drown me, but you
do not hear or
do not care and
I go on, trembling
because I do not understand.

Suzanne Brooks

POET

You think you are hidden
Behind dark glasses and a shrug.
But your fingers tightly gripping
The coffee cup that is no substitute
For the gin, reveal the fear that
We will find out what made you
Come; when all the time between
The last time, you fought the habit.
Your need is always for something
Stronger, though you don glibness
And hope no one will notice
How desperate you are for intoxication.

STOPS

In a station where no train
ever arrives, the modern poets
murmur and move without rhythm,
claiming it is confessional.
I have my own view of things.
It seeps out when I see where
I'm headed is only for a few.
Everybody ought to know their own
destiny, even if it's being left

back at the starting gate.

Suzanne Brooks

INS AND OUTS

All them nights
laying up & fucking,
You mumbling how
I lay back
puttin' all the work
on you and I
listened 'cause
after a while you
started making
sense in between
all them other
carrying-ons.

But just when
I got up
& got myself
a job and started
being Somebody,
You started
talking 'bout
women's responsibilities
and homeplace.
What side
of the bed
You on, anyway?

Slobber running
out side-mouth
round spit out words,
I rolled
my eyes back
thinking, this
man's crazy.

Looking at you
After a while, anybody'd
See I was right.
I did. So
I laughed inside
but some must
have slipped out
when I wasn't
looking for your fist.
But you missed, so
I ain't mad
at you walking out
thinking I'm putting on
a front you can
tear down to look
inside.

Too many tears done
already gone down.
Ain't nothing left
but another laugh.

Suzanne Brooks

CROSS

Worn round my neck,
if asked, I'd say
it wards off vampires;
but those thirsting
for my blood are not
deterred by such symbols

WOMAN SONG (FOR ARAY)

In a room of
sobbing people
I stare too long
Into the coffin
of this woman I
never knew.

Seated, I watch
the hypocrites.
They are easy to spot. They
always kiss the dead.

Aray, Aray,
you surely
deserved more
than this.

You are woman
dead, alone,
known only
by your husbands,
your children.

Men are remembered
by their work
and conquests.

They never cared
to know you.
I never can.

In this weeping crowd
only my tears are pure.

Suzanne Brooks

CHANGES (AS IN GOING THROUGH SOME)

If I holler
while I wallow
in the dirt
some'll say
I'm cool,
even though
they feel inside
I'm acting
like a fool.

If I'm yellow
or I mellow
with the years
or booze or pot,
I may sometimes
be disgraceful,
but unpopular
I'm not.

If I liberate
or educate
myself, nobody
cares.
Long
as I retain
my accent
and don't try
to put on airs.

But if I should
cease to stammer,
make my points
in proper grammar,
would my fans
then bigger grow
or say she's still
a nigger, though.

Suzanne Brooks

MOMENTS FOR CLAUDE WILLIAMS

So many poets I
love die without
knowing me and so you—
victim of jeering thoughts
and bitter tears in black
despondency in Spokane
in the sixties. But your moments live on
in my poems
because unlike so many
others, you had the guts
not to die by your own hand.

DECISIONS

Years after yielding
to pressure to make
the "right" decision
there is awful
agony in finding
You made the wrong
Decision anyway.
It is harder to live
with mistakes you
have been convinced
to make.

Suzanne Brooks

SONG OF AUTUMN IN SPRING

Youth, divine treasure,
already you go, never to return.
When I want to cry, I don't cry
and sometimes I cry without wanting to.

AFTER DIVORCE

Feelings placed on paper leave
Spaces to be filled. They are
The surest signals of an end.
We fell in love
With other people:
Long-haired me,
Boyish you.

The time has come to separate
The photographs, some to share,
The rest to hide from
Others and ourselves.

I will wear short hair
And bitten nails. For you
Songs sung will be out
Of tune. But here
Is the poem
You always wanted me
To write about you.

Suzanne Brooks

PILLOW TALK

The women watch
waiting for the word
and I am silent
not knowing how to soften
truth for those trained
to be pillows.

LONELINESS IS EXPENSIVE

Loneliness is expensive.
I pay for it in telephone calls
and long letters
with too many I's
to friends who also talk
only about themselves.
How easy it would be
to say we don't communicate,
but we do, we do.
We say "I am lonely
and tired, lonely and sad,
lonely but happy or
valuable or proud.

Suzanne Brooks

A WOMAN'S STUDY

Three hundred women, maybe more
sit encircled, trading
quips, which leave me unamused
but not unaffected while they
occasionally, obliquely touch
on our presence in the world
but not our absence from the room.

Three hundred women, maybe more
dressed in pants pretend
they are "new" women—some group
to which we (obviously) do not belong.
We are absent from this
study of women's lives,
are not these feminists made secure
by unpainted shelves piled high
with the junk that fills our houses.

And so I fail to find
nostalgia in their precious pieces
of poverty or meaning
in the word of those
yet to recognize our absence or demands.
These women, secure in their momentary
local majority, cling together
while we stand lonely in their midsts
but knowing we are only rejected
here and will survive
because each of us belongs more
to this Disney world than
all these three hundred women,
maybe more.

MIDLIFE CRISIS

I'm not sure when
or how it happened
but the day I realized
that I had probably
lived nearly, probably
at least half
of my life
I became afraid to die.
'Til then, I thought
forty was nothing but a number.
As I grow older
I grow more cowardly.

Suzanne Brooks

WAR GAMES

I could understand a war
begun by children raised
on cartoons and Pac-man.
They have reasons to believe
that war's a game
that ends electronically without
real damage and needs
only another coin to go
back to the beginning.
But what fool past forty
rushes forward to die,
doesn't feel hopelessly mortal.
Do we sacrifice our young
out of envy for their youth?

VALUE OF BELIEF

Once as a child,
I wanted to be a nun,
believed in miracles and more,
things unsustained in adulthood.

Now, after forty,
philosophies fail to comfort
my mounting fears
Of death approaching.

I grope for comfort in family
history—so few have died—but
they will and I will and
I don't want to.

Religious messages elude me
or muddle my thinking.
I believe nothing and everything.
I wear a cross.

I bathe in white flowers, feeling
pagan and guilty and uncertain.
Being agnostic is a lot more
comfortable before forty.

Suzanne Brooks

END NOTES

When you have really loved
And come to the final end
Of an affair, the feeling
Within is not so much
Of sadness or loneliness
As of emptiness.

The ties that bind
Another soul
Are stepping stones
Toward your goals.

And I mean nothing
Like the rest,
Only a stair where
You stopped to rest

Back again, that desire for music.
A torch song in B flat haunts me.
Back again, that longing for you.
Oh, to be free of your memory.

PALOUSE PALATE

The speeding car spurns
the stagnant view, urges
the horizon through a windshield
that reflects the greens
of growing grain. Harvest
Golds are still a season
away. Yet there is excitement
in this time of crop birth.
I pass an old farm and images
of closeness to land and man
fly out like birds scared
from nests. A man astride
a tractor on a hill
should have wide views
but those who have made this
northwest passage before are not
lulled by the rippling landw
which echoes still with cheers
for a King's murder. In this
white man's land crime is
any shade of brown,
so black just passes through
because everything dark
gets painted or run over.

Suzanne Brooks

WOUND POWER

"her wounds came from the same source as her power"
Adrienne Rich, *The Dream of a Common Language*

I got fucked by a white
who fucked my husband.
Afterward, I spent time
in the mirror wondering
if I should have kept
straightening my hair.
But not wanting to get
burnt again, I hung on
to my natural.

MARITAL STATUS

I shall have several husbands
for such is the way of a woman
of the world. Too simple
remaining single, so simple
to single out some man
as singular
but not for a lifetime.

Suzanne Brooks

HANDICAPPED

Disabilities last. Barren
Women take nothing for granted,
Make the best mothers. The more
Prolific think of territories.

The childless choose all children
As their own which is a thing
Best done silently. In moments
Of revelation there is too
Often misunderstanding.

I am the one, chosen to be
Deformed, mother of all
Deformity, bearing collective
Guilt in many guises,
Oracle of what is
Otherwise unspeakable.

All my children lie
Awake in the hideous
Dark. Beaten breathing
Whispers that they are there.
There is no light to show
Their numbers, too many
To count by recollection.

It is not impossible
To adjust to the death
of a child. At night there
Is always hope of young
Dreams and days bring other
Faces to search for semblances.

My dread is of the living
Like mongoloid Marian
With misshapen body and head.
Surely her slanted eyes see
Me cringe and turn away from
Her innocence. Her only
Shame Is what I show.

I visualized some fine future
For David that he will
Never see though I have
Looked for a cure for the blind-
ness that keeps me From seeing
The way to love him.

Lullabies are wasted on
Richard who never listens.
But though I have never
Called him dummy to his face,
He watches me as if
he reads my mind.

It is not as if
I am insensitive.
I am not the parent
They would have chosen
As they are not what
I expected. I am only
One and helpless. They
Are overwhelming.

They beat me down
and rob me of my hopes.
Theirs is the pity, not mine.
I lie at night, trapped in
The hush of suffering. If
I should die before I wake,
Will I have escaped?

Suzanne Brooks

What answer to what prayer
Would take them away without
Leaving me more alone to fear
The rest? They do not know that
They are mine. They *are*
Mine, a choice made
Against my will, that will
Not be sacrificed to save me.

ELEGY FOR A MILKMAN

We never spoke
All those days
Passing each other
On the stairs.
Your white truck
Parked outside
Seemed sterile.
I never wanted
To know you.
Then your scream
Roused me from
Restless sleep.
I answered reluctantly,
Not knowing it was you.

Through my window
Your empty truck,
Now quiet, now
Bloody, forces
Me to realize
How much we shared—
We, who are strangers.
And my own scream
Deep in my throat
Fails to call you.

Unknown name,
We are alike,
You and I.
We are afraid,
We are alike
Unwilling to die.
We are alike,
We are both victims—
You of the knife,
Me of indifference.

Suzanne Brooks

LOST FOR WORDS

An English major,
Who thinks of herself as a poet,
With much to say
But lacking the words not to show it,
Regrets the end of the class
Though it means
One more step has been made
Toward my goals, my dreams.
To best sum up my journal, I chose
The words of another poet to close.

From T.S. Eliot, "The Love Song of J. Alfred Prufock"
And indeed there will be time
To wonder, "Do I dare?" And "Do I dare? . . .
Do I dare disturb the universe? . . .
I have seen the moment of my greatness flicker
I have seen the eternal Footman hold my coat, and snicker
And in short, I was afraid.
And would it have be worth it, after all . . .?

REFLECTIONS

She comes between us
Like another woman. I
See the threat she poses
You blind eyes: she
Walks like me.

She whispers in your ear
The way I used to. I
See you smile at echoes
In your mind: she
Talks like me.

She has the laugh
You only shared
With me in the days
Before your dimples
Marked her cheeks.

My chunky shortness
Stretches taut in her,
Exposing what I would
Be, were I not me.

The day the children leave
Comes all too soon.
Your tears will be
So different from my own.

Suzanne Brooks

PICTURES

Kemo-sabe laughed at
Tonto's fear of cameras
But Tonto was right,
Photographs capture the spirit
And three stuffed albums
Can sum up a life.

Within a green cover
Baby pictures yellow
From age and paste.
The chubby held-out hands
Give no hint of the pale puffs
Now wiping wedding book dust.

White laced smiles
Pledged to last a lifetime
Held only until the middle
Of the last book of houses
And Christmas trees and
New babies with old faces.

Someday, someone will glance
Through these albums, hoping
To find some of the old gloss. All
That will be seen is the faded
Spirit of those we do not recognize
But who reflect ourselves.

THE STORIES

Suzanne Brooks

A FAMILY TREE

The town is only one mile square with a main road that dips as it moves south, then rises five miles later to another hill. Looking back from there, the court house can be seen exactly centered on the hilltop. In spring the marble columns seem to float on the trees, lording it over the town now hidden in the foliage. Two blocks behind the courthouse, on a treeless corner, sits the First Baptist Church. A grey stone building, surrounded by high black fence, it is the real center of justice and judgment.

On Sunday mornings, when the pastor opens the door for services, all but the first row of pews fill quickly. The front row, however, is reserved for the deacons' board whose members enter together just before the start of services. They are the controlling powers, these men in the front row. To them, the man in the pulpit is only a hired hand.

According to the old wives' tale, the preacher's son is always the worst behaved child in any community. But the preacher of the First Baptist Church was not yet married. He was therefore presumed to be childless. Perhaps to make up for the absence of the usual target of concern, the local gossips paid more attention to Marian Moffet whose father was president of the deacons' board. The location of the Moffet house, right across from the church, kept porch-sitting Marian in constant view so that she made up for what she lacked in looks and talent by what she offered in easy accessibility.

It is not easy to tell your mother that you are pregnant at any age. It is harder when you are fifteen and the deacon's daughter. But somehow Marian had managed that much. After a few "Lord, Lord's," her mother, Mrs. Moffet got down to business.

"Who's is it?"

"Oliver's."

"Y'all wanna get married?"

"He don't. Said I oughta get rid of it. Sides, Daddy'll have a fit, he finds out." Her tongue flicked over pale, flaky lips at the thought of her father's reaction: endless preaching and praying.

"Stop licking your mouth. How you let this happen?" The mother tugged at the lopsided dress that struggled to cover an immense rear, then dumped herself onto the sofa.

58

"Just happened. You goin' help me?" Mrs. Moffett studied her daughter's red-brown face, bland except for the pimpled forehead. This day had been coming for a long time. The girl was big-legged and big-chested, but small brained. Wasn't her fault.

"Guess there ain't nothing' else to do. Your daddy in the church an' all. Just don't say nothing' 'bout this to nobody." She rocked back and closed her eyes. The red velvet couch creaked on its spindly legs. Marian flipped the pages of a comic book while her mother thought things out. Soon, the mother opened her eyes and leaned forward.

"I know somebody in Sharon Hill to do it. A lady. You take off school. We tell your daddy Aunt Ethel's sick an' needs you t'help out a while." The case closed, she struggled up from the couch. Marian looked up.

"When I'm goin'?"

"Tomorrow." Marian looked back at her lap and went on reading.
She took the morning bus to Sharon Hill. The *lady* lived walking distance from the bus stop. Marian found the place easily. It was a row-house with an enclosed porch. Worn green shades covered the paint-peeling windows. The lady, Miss Gladys, was younger than Marian expected. She wondered how her mother knew this woman in shiny gold loungewear that matched the light brown skin and testified to the lucrativeness of her business.

"You Marian?"

"Uh huh. My mother called you?"

"Yeah, come on in." Miss Gladys led the way to a back room. A wooden chair, an army cot with a bare mattress and an old metal cabinet furnished it.

"Sit down." Miss Gladys waved toward the chair. "I got some stuff to do first." Marian sat. There was nothing to say. From the cabinet came a long red rubber tube with a wire hanging out the end, a pair of gloves and a pile of newspaper. The woman covered the mattress with paper, tucking it under the edges, then turned back to the girl.

"Take off your pants and your shoes. You can keep on your socks if you want. Then lay down over here." Hesitating, Marian asked,

"Will it hurt?"

"Yeah, but you'll live. Hurry up."

59

Undressed, Marian lowered herself gingerly onto the cot. She held her legs together tightly as she stretched out. Miss Gladys put on the rubber gloves.

"Move your legs."

Marian saw the wired tube in the gloved hands. She opened her legs. Miss Gladys bent over and pushed the girl's thighs wider with one hand. She felt the girl's stomach with her palm for a second, then with a practiced finger probed the vagina. Marian turned her head aside and closed her eyes. Quickly, Miss Gladys withdrew the finger and replaced it with the tube. Marian sucked in a breath.

"That's the first part. You stay here. I'll be back." She left the room, shutting the door behind her. Marian lay on the bed, relieved that her father would not find out. God knows she wasn't the first girl to ever get pregnant. She chuckled to herself. "God knows, but Daddy doesn't." She thought back to the night she sneaked out with Oliver. Smiling, she fell asleep.

When she woke, it was night. In the dark, she did not remember where she was. A sudden cramp in her stomach refreshed her memory. The door opened. The light was switched on. Shielding her eyes from the glare, she saw Miss Gladys with a glass,

"Something for you to drink. A laxative. You feeling anything? Drink it all." Marian sipped from the glass and grimaced. "My stomach hurts." She gulped the rest of the liquid without breathing.

"Good. That means you're started." Miss Gladys took back the glass. "I'll be back in an hour." When she was gone, Marian tried going back to sleep, but the nagging pain inside kept her alert. The light bothered her eyes even when she shut them. A muscle in her leg tightened. She shifted on the cot, but the movement added to her discomfort. She decided to stay still. When her back began to ache, she tried to sit up. Pain knifed across her stomach as if something were being torn away. She struggled for breath and lay down again. The calves of her legs hardened. She tried stretching out. This made her feet cramp. Feeling something wet, she touched her inner thighs. When she raised her hand, it was bloody. Vomit rose in her throat. Gasping for air, she swallowed hard. Contractions began. She rolled on her side, holding her stomach with her arms and brought her knees up close to her chest. Fear wrenched tears from her eyes. She tore off a piece of the paper near her head. With it, she wiped at the mucus seeping from her nose. At last, not knowing what else to do, she screamed. Miss Gladys appeared in the doorway.

"Guess you're ready now. It'll be over soon." Marian prayed for something to kill the pain. Miss Gladys examined her. The wire was yanked from the tube. Marian screamed again.

"Listen, Marian. It hurts, but you can't let the whole world know what's happening. Cut the noise!" The patient nodded. Miss Gladys examined her again. A look of dismay replaced her previous confidence.

"Something's a little wrong. It's not coming out right. You're pretty far gone. I gotta turn it around. You're gonna have to hang tough." Marian's fear gave way to stark terror. God was punishing her after all. Miss Gladys went back to the cabinet and took out some rolls of gauze and tape. She stuffed Marian's mouth with the gauze and taped across it. Marian hoped to pass out. Pushing outside the girl's stomach with one hand and inside with the other, Miss Gladys grappled for the head of the fetus. Muffled moans oozed through the gauze. Perspiration dripped from the woman onto the girl. Blood soaked the newspapers until with a jerk, the soft, pulpy mass was pulled free. Marian fainted.

By morning, she felt tired and weak but the pain was gone. Miss Gladys brought her some oatmeal.

"You got to eat to get your strength. You go home tomorrow. Next time be more careful."

"I ain't goin' through this again. If it's a next time, I guess my daddy'll just have to fuss." Marian looked out the window and saw that snow had fallen during the night. She tried to forget about the present by thinking about the coming spring.

There are no trees around the First Baptist Church. No one notices this because the hedges inside the fence are thick and high. By June the leaves on the bushes are woven into a dense curtain that separates the church from its surroundings. Late on a June night, Marian walked stealthily through the gate into the church yard. She was not surprised when the custodian's son James stepped out to meet her.

"Hey, Marian."

"That you, James?" She squinted into the shadows

"Who else?" He laughed softly.

"I don't know."

"Oh, come on. I was kiddin'. I got the keys. Lets go." He led the way to the church door and unlocked it. The pair stepped into the inner darkness. With exaggerated tiptoeing, they-made their way to the front of the church.

"You still giving me some, Marian?"

"Said I was didn't I?" The momentary lovers moved into a pew. In a brown tangle of arms and legs, the next spring's crop was sewn. Across the street from the church, Deborah Moffet was born at home in March.

The Moffet house seems aloof in its spot on the hill. It is a faded rather than pale, green. Windowless on the east and west, it stands unprepared to meet the cold north winds. In front, it sits level with the ground like other houses about town. But in back, the land drops away sharply—a small cliff looking down onto an empty lot. It is as if the land has sucked in its belly, retreated to avoid touching.

For Deborah, the house was a silent sanctuary with no sounds of its own—only those made by its few occupants.

She felt, rather than heard her grandfather's shuffle across the wooden porch and the rattle of windows in a storm. She could not remember her grandmother, dead before she was four. Her earliest recollection was of her mother and Pop Pop saying something she couldn't hear all of and still knowing that their talk was about her. It didn't matter that she'd missed those words. In time, the gaps were filled in—overfilled—so that she would switch off her hearing aid and refuse to listen. The words went on anyway.

"Likely it's the Lord's way a' doin'," Mr. Moffet always began. Now in her twenties, but already showing signs of a coming middle age spread, Marian watched him fondle a small, brown-paper covered Bible. She had looked at it once but, finding it without pictures, lost interest in the possibility of reading it.

"Your mother, this chil's gran'mother," he pointed to Deborah, "wasn't no smart woman, for sure. But it don't take smartness to get along n'all. Being in the church, she was a good woman. You lis'nin', Marian?" He paused without looking up from his lap.

"I hear you," Marian answered in monotone. From anyone else, the words would have been sarcastic, but from Marian they were simply a statement of fact. She could not have said she understood without lying and she was incapable of thinking beyond truth. Satisfied that he had an audience, the old man bobbed his head. The yellowish-gray hair circling his bald pate reminded Marian of a halo or one of those leafy things from the gladiator comics.

"Bein's your mother was on the slow side, it wasn't no surprise you took after her," continued Mr. Moffet.

Marian looked at her hands and found a broken fingernail. "I'm like Mama, Debbie's like me," she droned, anxious for the sermon to end so she could fix her nails.

"Thought so when she's little. 'Til we found out she's deaf."

Deborah looked around from the television with its volume turned all the way down. The movement of her head exposed mute figures on the screen that seemed to peek around the sides of her brown, bushy hair.

"I ain't deaf, Pop Pop. Else a hearin' aid wouldn' do me no good." She resumed watching the pantomime, again oblivious to the others.

"Whatever," replied the withered man as if to Marian.
"Might be she has some luck comin' for it. That's the Lord's way a' doin'. Long's you put your hands in the hands..."

"Of the man from Galilee," finished Marian.

If she had been capable of reflection, Mr. Moffet's remarks would have induced Marian to think about her mother. Mrs. Moffet had loved that spiritual and had sung it whenever she was happy. When things were going bad, like the winter of the bus strike when she had walked to her housecleaning job, she turned the melody into a kind of down home blues. When she was angry or in church on Sunday mornings, she sang it like Gabriel giving out the judgment on everybody. But all anybody ever said about her singing was, "You sure do love that song." It was a way of not telling her you got tired of hearing that tuneless rasp over and over. And though the song didn't change, the voice did, from cigarette hoarseness to a tubercular laryngitis. She died soon after she stopped singing.

Marian accepted her mother's death but not the inconvenience of her mother's absence. Mrs. Moffet had been the one who took care of Deborah. Back home after the funeral, Marian questioned her father.

"Who' s gonna take care of Debbie now?"

"You her mother. Ain' nobody else."

"But I never took care of her before. Sides, I'm s'posed to go job training in the city." Marian spoke in her usual matter of fact way. She had

63

interpreted a social worker's suggestion as an order. As she saw it, she *had* to go.

"Guess I forgot." Mr. Moffet nodded while he rocked in his chair. "No use to worrying. You go on. Debbie'll be here till you get back. We'll be all right, I guess." And suddenly missing the wife he had lived with for so long, he remembered the song she had sung. The words ran across his mind. He was unaware when he spoke out loud.

"Put your hand in the hands of the man from Galilee."

Disgusted, Marian got up from her chair and went upstairs to pack.

Deborah's school days had not begun until she was eight—the mandatory age under state law. Not knowing she was hard of hearing her mother and grandfather assumed her stumbling language was the result of some brain trouble. Had he known about his daughter's abortion, Mr. Moffet would have said it was a judgment of God. But he never knew.

Mental illness was still shameful, so Deborah was kept hidden until a school attendance officer ordered her sent to training school. In her five weeks at Elgin Institute, Deborah was tested, found to be bright but hard of hearing and fitted with a hearing aid. Then she returned home. Mr. Moffet was advised to enroll her in the public school or face a stiff fine. The next day, eight year old Deborah began first grade. Four years later, she had progressed enough to be shipped into sixth grade.

She would always remember Miss Holly, her sixth grade teacher. This pock-faced woman, with middle-aged spread, snarled the class to order each day. But Deborah found a soft spot in the tough hide. Miss Holly loved underdogs and Deborah's history made her a rare breed. At the end of the school year, the teacher talked with her pet.

"What're you doing for the summer, Debbie?"

"Nothin'," the girl answered.

"If I could arrange it with your folks, would you like to go to camp? You could play with other children, sing, swim, and lots of other things."

"I can't swim," said Deborah, looking down at her feet.

"Then you'd learn. What do you think? Like to go?" The teacher smiled, nearly cracking the habitually rigid face.

"Maybe it cost too much. We're kinda poor." The voice seeped from under the bowed head.

"No, no. It won't cost your family anything. Well?"

"I never went any place for real, Miss Holly. I sure would like goin'."
"Then it's settled. You'll go."

And Miss Holly, long practiced in dictating the lives of sixth graders, with no trouble, got permission for Deborah to go.

The trip was not at all what Deborah expected. She had imagined riding through miles of dense woods, but in fact, when the trees of the town the road rambled through the rolling hills laden with yet to be harvested wheat. To Deborah, unused to seeing large expanses of land without trees, it seemed naked.

From the bus window, she looked down the sides of the road into gulleys fanning out into farmland and wondered how the road always managed to be set up higher than the fields. She had not known there were so many other shades of green as she now saw. Unused to animals, she marveled at the occasional lone horse or the small groups of grazing cows. Then the road dipped unexpectedly and for a few seconds the bus was airborne. Inside, Deborah was lifted from her seat. Her eyes focused upward, and for the first time she saw that there is more sky than earth. She was not conscious of falling back to the seat. The bus passed streams and jagged cliffs. Deborah tilted her seat back and stared skyward into the endless blue. This was a trip to remember. She was sure she would not forget it. In the distance a grove of trees came in view. Deborah looked down and saw the wooden sign announcing the entrance to the camp.

Camp Wissonoming, named for the lake beside it, was fifty miles from the house across from the First Baptist Church. Deborah loved the lake which was fed by warm and cold springs. She learned to row the rough wooden boats back and forth across the green, placid water. Afternoons, she lay back in her boat, staring at the sky or clouds or birds, secure in the knowledge that she could drift about without danger because the lake had only underground outlets.

But it was *in* the water that she felt most alive. She learned to swim quickly, naturally, like some young untamed animal. The budding sensuality of adolescence was stirred by the alternating pressures of springs spouting below the surface, against her body. When she caught a cold from staying out too long, she ignored it, wiping her runny nose on her hand and rinsing it in the water. Infection spread to her already weak ears. She did not hear again.

In September, Deborah was transferred to Central School for the Deaf. In the philosophy of the school, *even* the deaf could be taught something. Deborah was enrolled in the sewing curriculum. The only other option—printing—was reserved for boys.

On the first day, Deborah followed the other 13 year olds to class. Having little mechanical dexterity she dreaded the sewing courses. Entering the room, she was happily surprised to discover herself surrounded by desks rather than work tables. The teacher, Miss Hansen, sat at her own desk in front, waiting for the students to settle down. When they were all seated Miss Hansen walked to the blackboard, picked up a piece of chalk and began writing in large letters: BALL, B B B ALL ALL ALL BALL BALL BALL .

All around Deborah, students pulled out headsets from desks and put them on. She looked inside her own desk and followed suit. Miss Hansen thumped the floor with her foot. The class became still. Miss Hansen pointed to the first word, sucked in her lips and blew out "*BBAALLL.*" Deborah heard an undistinguishable noise through the earphones. The teacher moved to the first B, reformed her lips and said "Buh, buh, buh." She beckoned to the class. Thirty voices repeated variations of Buh, buh, buh. Deborah saw their lips move and pretended to follow suit. She wondered what the purpose of this exercise was. She already knew how to sound a B. After twenty minutes of "Buh, buh, buh," Deborah's mind began to wander. She tried peering out the window, but sat too low to see over the sill. Then she felt vibrations on her desk. Looking up, she saw Miss Hansen pounding it with a ruler. The teacher signaled for Deborah to hold out her hands. She held them gingerly forward. Her deafness spared her the sound of the ruler cutting through the air, though not the blow that followed

Miss Hansen returned to the front of the room, but kept an eye on Deborah. The lesson resumed. Deborah sounded, "Buh, buh, buh; all all all; ball ball ball ball," for the rest of the week. By the following week, sewing seemed a relief. Six years later, it was a habit. Given a certificate of completion, she was sent home—a better than average seamstress. Her speech completely reformed, she could no longer articulate even the simplest word. She arrived home feeling shut out of the hearing world completely and forever.

The house had not changed in her absence. Her mother had never returned from the city and by the time Deborah was twenty-five, her grandfather had been sent, senile, to a rest home to wait for the last time to put his hand in the hands of the man from Galilee. The house became Deborah's. Some time after, Deborah became pregnant. No one knew the father. No one asked or cared. But with Ruth's birth, she was no longer alone. On this child, named from her grandfather's bible, Deborah poured the love she had never shared. She was an angel, this Ruth, with golden skin and hair, and soft gray eyes. She would fly high some day. And though her daughter's gray eyes could harden like the rocks on the back yard ledge, when it came to Ruth, Deborah was more blind than deaf.

"Don' care y'are my mother. I hate you, dummy," Ruth screamed at her mother's back as she had for half of her twelve years. Deborah continued ironing unhearing and so undisturbed. Ruth turned away in disgust. Outside the kitchen window, the small yard was dark. A dim light from the lot below silhouetted the old cherry tree which grew in the space between the house and the cliff ledge. Ruth pushed the curtain aside. Her old swing hung motionless. She fanned the warm air into her eyes.

"Ru, Ru." Her mother's voice drew her unwilling attention back into the room. Deborah clasped hands together, as in prayer, then raised them to her tilted head in the sign for sleep. Bedtime. For *other* people, the quiet end of the day. But here with a deaf mother, it was always quiet. Ruth nodded understanding, then went upstairs.

Inside her room, she thought about Janice Benton. Janice went to the hairdresser and had her own horse. She thought she was better than everybody else. And all those other kids, hanging around Janice, hoping she'd take them for a ride. But she never did.

She hated Janice. Even so, stepping on Janice's foot in the school lunchroom had been an accident.

"Hey! That's my foot," Janice had yelled. Ruth said nothing.

"Well, you could say you're sorry," Janice commanded.

"It wasn't on purpose."

"Say it anyway."

"No." Ruth picked up her lunch tray and started for a table.

"You just wait," Janice threatened. Ruth unloaded her tray at a corner table. At the next table, Janice held court with four admirers. Ruth opened her milk.

"Rururu." It was a girl's voice. Ruth shut her eyes. That again. She heard giggling and spun to see the speaker. The five girls were now eating silently, without looking up. Ruth returned to her 'lunch.

"Rururuth." A different voice.

Again Ruth faced them. Again they pretended not to notice her. Ruth turned away.

"Dis is Yuh muddah, Ruru." Loud laughter joined the lone voice. Ruth knew the old routine. On and on, until they drove her away. She left the lunchroom and headed for the school yard to wait until time for class.

There, in her desk, she found a note.

"Your mother is a dummy."

Ruth put it in her blouse pocket. If she tore it up, they'd send another. Now as she undressed for bed, she felt the note beneath the soft material. She took it out and read it a last time.

In bed with the light out, Ruth planned. The twenty-seven dollars in her bank would buy a bus ticket and leave some left for food. She'd get a job. She looked older. Maybe babysitting. She could do that. Or ironing.

Her thoughts were interrupted by a thump—her mother putting the ironing board away. Heavy footsteps on the stairs warned that her mother was going to bed, too. Ruth closed her eyes and lay still. Her door creaked open and for a second, the hall light shone on her face. Then her mother's thumping steps moved away. Ruth tried to remember when her mother had begun walking like that.

At the sound of snoring, she got out of bed.

She dressed, emptied her school bag, then packed her money, a sweater, her comb and brush. She tiptoed past her mother's door, down the steps, and out of the house.

Deborah stared past the raised shade. The sun which usually woke her had not yet arisen. The fitfulness of the night's sleep carried over into the fatigue she now felt.

But if she couldn't sleep, she might as well get up, Deborah thought about her daughter. ("Ru good girl. Strong. Pretend no bother. Kids make fun Ru mother. Too much worry Ru.") Deborah put on her robe. ("Time Ru wake. Give pancake breakfast. Ru like.")

"Ru-Ru. Ru-Ru." She rumbled toward Ruth's room.

"Ruru." She pushed the door open. The empty bed confused her. She turned and headed for the bathroom, but stopped when she saw the door open, the light off. She lumbered downstairs.

"Ru?" From room to room, no answer. ("Ru, where? Can't hear. Something happen? Maybe Ru call mother help.") Deborah grabbed a coat and put it on over her robe. ("Police find Ru.") She ran out the door.

The police station was across town. Deborah ran all the way. She stumbled through the doors, exhausted and gasping for breath. Inside, she clung to the information counter for support. A policeman approached.

"Help you ma'am?'

"Ru. Ru-Ru," she answered, her voice more garbled than ever by shortness of breath.

"What'd you say?" Her answer confused him.

"Ru-Ru." She grabbed a ticket book from the counter and moved her hand as if writing.

"You deef?" the officer asked, pointing to his ear. She nodded. He handed her a notepad. She scribbled, "Ruth daughter gone no home mother wake up gone." She shoved the note at him.

"I get it." He nodded as he spoke.

"Better get a seat though. You don't look so good. Hell, you can't hear me. Wait a minute." He raised his hand signaling her to stay where she was, while he walked around to her side. As he moved away, a crash sounded. He rushed to the woman now sprawled on the floor. Grabbing her wrist, he tried to find a pulse. Nothing. Kneeling, he bent his head to her chest. There was nothing to hear. Slowly, he got up. Behind the counter again, he dialed the phone.

"This is Minter. Woman just collapsed here. I think she's dead..."

At dawn, the bus station is as quiet as the rest of the town. Morning buses do not begin rolling until 7 a.m. Covered by her sweater, Ruth slept soundly on a bench in the ladies room. Sudden, loud banging jolted her awake.

"Anybody in there?" A man's voice.

Ruth found herself afraid to answer.

More banging.

"Janitor here. Comin' in for the trash."

'Wait a minute," Ruth called out with relief. She picked up her school bag. Opening the door she saw an old man. His back bent with the weight of a huge sack.

"What you doin' there girl?"

"Goin' to the bathroom." She relaxed even more. He didn't know her.

"Look like you playin' hooky." He grinned toothlessly.

"No, I ain't," she answered hotly.

"Tha's good 'cause then you ain't that girl the police is lookin' for."

Ruth looked down at her feet to avoid the eyes that stared at her. The janitor went on talking. "Police came round, while ago. Said if I see any girl run'way to let 'em know. Sumpin' happen to her mother." The grinning face looked evil.

"Somethin' happened, like what?"

"What you care for? Less'n you the girl?"

"Just askin', That's all."

"Don' know 'xactly, but if'n I was the girl, I'd git on home 'n find out."

Ruth ambled toward the street door. She stepped outside, then began to run. Behind her, ugly laughter faded as she fled.

The front door of the Moffet house was wide open—unusual for her mother who was always afraid of someone walking in without her knowing it. Ruth ran inside. She slammed the door hard and waited for her mother to respond to the vibrations. The sound was swallowed by the silence. She searched the house. Her mother's bed was still unmade. She decided to check the basement. The coat rack in the cellarway caught her eye. Her mother's coat was gone.

"Must be out lookin' for me," Ruth mumbled to herself. She decided to wait.

70

Opening the back door, Ruth saw her old swing. She didn't use it much anymore, but it'd be something to do till her mother got back. Her feet pushed against the dirt for a good start. She swung out over the cliff. When she had been very young, the drop from this swing had seemed endless. Now she saw how really short the depth was. Her back arched. She pumped higher. Her mother had made this swing. Ruth worked her legs. The swing rose higher. Over the roof she could see the walls of the First Baptist Church, stiff like the robes of a merciless judge. The church made her think suddenly of the paper-covered bible in which her mother had found her name. She knew the story of the loving daughter whose words said something about going wherever the mother went. From far below, a policeman's voice called out.

"Ruth, you have to come down."

LIGHT THROUGH THE IVY

Two blocks north of the courthouse, the Jackson house was built more than a hundred years ago by Marie Jackson's runaway slave grandparents. Marie was born there. When she was young, Marie called it a "freedom 'house." The house is still there. Its wooden porch sags against the crumbling bricks. Marie is still there too.

The front of the house faces the east to catch the morning sun. On the south side, crawling vines of ivy are woven into a mat that has to be cut away from the windows to let in the light.

There are no windows on the north side, just plain brick wall. Behind an iron fence across the street, the First Baptist Church towers over the house. Nothing else is left from the old neighborhood.

Like the house, Marie has three sides. Before her first child was born, she was vivacious and popular. Next, she became "Mama," a devoted, doting parent. Her marriage wrought the last change. Now she's like the north side of the house, that blank unchanging wall. The sag of age is hardly visible on this side.

Though she loved her child's father and spoke of him as a "sweet Daddy," Marie never said his name. Why? He had a wife. He refused to get a divorce and marry her. The affair ended painfully, but not quietly. Like most small towns, Media thrived on gossip. The stories grew with Marie's pregnancy. The women whispered.

"Never thought Marie was 'that' kind of girl."

"Always puttin' on airs. Like she's better'n the rest of us. Serves her right."

"Wonder who the father is?"

"From what I heard, it could be anybody."

Still, Marie's beauty made men catch their breath. Only now their eyes leered when she walked by. The tone of their voices changed.

"What happened, Marie? Swallow a watermelon seed?"

'No, she was in an accident. Somebody hit and run."

They laughed.

72

Marie retreated into the house. Her daughter, Joette, was born there. Before long, Marie nicknamed her "Sugar." She was the sweetness of Marie's life. Nothing, no one else mattered. Not until Dave.

Dave was eight years old when his mother tired of Georgia sharecropping and came north. Dave, his sister— Chi-Chi, and one old suitcase were all she had. No friends and no money. Somehow, she found an old shack near the Media waterworks. The rent was a dollar a week. It was better than nothing, but not much.

Mrs. Davidson took in wash. Sometimes she scrubbed floors. There was never enough money. One day, the rent was raised to two dollars. Things got worse. They had no food. Mrs. Davidson took to sleeping with men, white ones mostly. After that, times began to get better for them.

She saved her money and kept away from the townspeople. Dave and Chi-Chi started school. Things did not get better there. Their classmates were cruel.

"Trash. Plain nigger trash."

"You gonna be a whore like your mother, Chi-Chi?"

The brother and sister faced the gang of children in the schoolyard. Chi-Chi's eyes filled with tears. She wiped her nose with her sleeve. Dave took off his jacket and shoved it in his sister's arms. She squeezed it against her chest .

"Go home, Chi:-Chi," Dave said. She didn't move. "I'll be okay. Don't worry. Just go, so I don't have to worry 'bout you." He pushed her away.

"Yeah, Chi-Chi. Go home to your mother," a boy yelled. "She's prob'ly there f...," Dave's fist stopped the rest, but only for the moment.

When she had saved enough money, Mrs. Davidson bought a truck. She and her children began to haul things for people. They made good. Soon, she hired a man to work for her. Then two. Then four. Slowly, she built a business. Davidson's Moving and Hauling. She moved her family to a better house. Then they joined the church. They became the most religious people in town. Never missed a Sunday service. Always ready to testify. The Davidsons were saved. They were going to save the world from sin, too. Whether the world liked it or not.

That's how Dave first saw Marie. He came out of that church across the street and saw her sitting on the front porch. He got it in his mind to "save" her.

Sugar and her mother don't get along with each other anymore. It's really all there in the word "Mother." Way back, when Sugar used to call her "Mama," she thought Marie loved her. Sugar was all that remained of the great love of Marie's life. When Marie was especially pleased with her daughter, she would say,

"Sugar, you're just like your daddy—sweetness and light." There were just the two of them, then.

When Marie first met Dave, things were still okay. He brought Sugar toys and sent her outside to play. Or, he gave somebody money to take her to the movies, while he stayed in the house with Marie. One afternoon, Marie told Sugar, "Me and Dave are getting married. We'll be a real family, Sugar. You can carry the flowers at the wedding."

Well, it was really fine—the wedding. Marie wore a light blue dress. It looked pretty against her coffee colored skin. Sugar was all in yellow because Marie said it matched her hair. The reception was held in the church hall. A lot of people were there.

Sugar was having a good time running around, playing hide 'n seek with her cousins Jimmy, Tinker and Earl, when she saw Marie and Dave talking to Dr. Willard. She always liked Dr. Willard, so she thought she'd talk to him too. They didn't see her walk behind them. Not allowed to interrupt "grown-ups" talking, she just stood there and listened, waiting for them to finish. Dave put his arm around Marie's waist.

"How you like my pretty new bride, Doc?"

"Oh, Dave!" Marie leaned over and kissed his smooth ebony cheek.

"A beauty, all right." Dr. Willard nodded his head. "You're a lucky man. Guess it won't be long before I'm delivering a new baby, huh?"

"Yeah, Doc, but it won't be another yellow girl. Or I'll know what's up." They all laughed.

"Gotta get to the hospital now. See you later." Dr. Willard walked toward the door. Sugar didn't follow him. Instead, she pulled Marie's arm.

"Don't you want any more little girls?"

"Yes, Sugar. We do. We were just kidding with the Doc. Big people's talk," Marie said. Dave grabbed Sugar's hand. He walked her over to the punch bowl and gave her a drink.

"Go on back to your playing. Forget about trying to understand grown-ups."

That was when Sugar was five.

In the months right after the wedding, things seemed about the same between Marie, Dave and Sugar. Almost. The only noticeable change was that Sugar had more freedom because Dave sent her out to play whenever he was home. Then Marie got pregnant. She looked forward to the arrival of the new baby. She wanted to please Dave. Sugar wanted a playmate. Dave said,

"Now I'll be a 'real' father." When Sunday came, the three of them went to church across the street. Dave stood up and told the congregation about his good luck, how he had been blessed. Sugar got sleepy while he was talking. Marie pinched her to keep her awake. After the long, long service, they went home.

Marie fixed a special dinner to celebrate. Ribs and greens for Dave. Lemon pie for Sugar. With a new tablecloth and the "good" dishes, the kitchen looked almost like a dining room. During the meal, Marie said,

"Sugar, when the baby comes, you won't be having all my time. There'll be a lot to do. Suppose we have a party for your birthday? After that you won't be the baby anymore."

"I'd like that, Mama."

"I'll make you a cake, too. What kind do you want?"

"Is it just up to me?"

"It's your birthday."

"Lemon pie. That's what I like."

"Who ever heard of pie for a birthday?" Dave interrupted. "Besides, Marie, you oughta wait for another time. The baby's almost due."

"No, it's not, Dave. I have almost another month to go. It'll be okay." She looked pleadingly at her husband. He just shrugged. Then as an afterthought, he added,

75

"If you gotta make something, it out to be a cake, like people usually have. Just 'cause she likes lemon pie, don't mean everybody does."

"I guess you're right about that. We'll compromise, Sugar, and have cake for the party," Marie said. Sugar nodded, afraid her voice would reveal the small disappointment if she spoke. Marie continued with the party plans.

"You can invite fifteen of your friends. Let's make a list." Marie took a note pad and pencil from the cabinet next to the table and began writing.

"First, Earl and Jimmy," said Sugar. "Then Sandy. Colleen and Sean...,"

"Wait a minute," Dave interrupted again. "Those are white names. Who's Colleen and Sean?"

"My friends. They ain't white. They're Miss Frances' kids," Sugar retorted.

"Sugar, we'll finish this later," Marie interjected quickly. "You go out and play now."

Sugar left the table and went out the back door into the yard. Dave glared at Marie. His lips were drawn tightly together. He waited until Sugar was gone before speaking.

"Let's get one thing straight, Marie. Those half-white kids not gonna come in this house long as I'm here. That Frances don't do nothing' but mess around white men. Her kids come here, that's a reason for y'all to start being around each other too."

"So what's that prove?" Anger edged into Marie's voice.

"You know how people talk. See you and Frances together, they'll be lookin' at Sugar and figure you're both the same."

"Could say it anyway. Everybody knows Sugar ain't yours."

"I don't need you to make me remember that. I hear all the talk. My mother hears it too."

"So what! Just as much talk about her. And I know all that story."

The words had been inside her for a long time, but Marie had not meant to say them. Not even in anger. Dave covered his face with his hands for a moment. Marie watched him in silence. When he removed his hands, his expression was like that of a captive African warrior, proud but defeated. His voice cracked.

"Do anything you want with Sugar, but don't ask me to do it with you. And don't ever tell me what you 'know' 'bout my mother." Without waiting for Marie's reply, he left the table and the room. The subject was closed. She walked to the back door and called outside.

"Sugar! Come back in and let's finish the party list."

When the day of the party came at last, Sugar was excited. She kept having to go to the bathroom. She ran upstairs for the fourth time. It was one o'clock. The party was to start at two. Before she could shut the bathroom door, she heard Marie's voice.

"Sugar! Sugar! Come quick!" The voice sounded funny. It scared her. She ran back down the stairs. Marie sat on a chair in the front room.

"Go next door. Tell Mrs. Wise to come over. Right away."

"What's the matter?"

"Later, Sugar. Go get Mrs. Wise."

The girl ran out the back door and across the yard between the two houses. The back door of the Wise house was never locked. She opened it and called inside.

"Mrs. Wise! Mrs. Wise! Mama says come over right away."

"Okay, Sugar. I'm coming." Mrs. Wise trailed her back to the Jackson house and Marie, who was still in the chair.

"Is it time, Marie?"

"Yes." The other woman nodded. "Sugar..." The front door opened suddenly and slammed against the wall. Sweating and breathing hard, Dave came inside. Marie continued, "I'm sorry. The baby's coming. I won't be here for your party."

"Mrs. Wise, take Sugar to your house," said Dave. "She'll have to have the party later. The car's out front, Marie.

Let's go."

He took his wife's arm and led her out the door. Through the window, Sugar watched them drive away. That was the day her brother, Joel, was born. She never did have a party. She thought she'd never be able to forgive Joel for that.

When Marie came home from the hospital with Joel, Sugar was disappointed by her first look at the small, wrinkled, brown ball that had canceled her party.

But as time went by, Joel didn't look so bad after all. A year later, when he first tried to call her name, she thought he was the prettiest baby in the world. It was easy to see why Dave fussed over him so. It wasn't easy to understand that time Dave fussed about Sugar.

It was on a hot August day. The summer was almost over. In a few days, September and third grade would arrive. Dave still worked for his mother as a mover. Often he came home late for dinner. Marie and Sugar listened to the radio on those nights. Joel always fell asleep in his playpen, but Marie never put him to bed until Dave got home. About eight o'clock, Dave came in. Marie was seated on the sofa.

"Hi!" He smiled at Marie, but didn't seem to notice Sugar.

"Hi! You hungry?" Dave looked at Joel as he slept.

"Yeah. Look, Marie! Looks just like me. Ain't that just the sweetest brown baby you ever saw?"

"Next one will be just as sweet," answered Marie.

"What next one?" Sugar looked at her mother for an answer. "Are we getting another baby?

Dave whirled to face the girl.

"Nobody's talking to you. Stop looking down my throat and go to bed."

Sugar started toward the stairs.

"Sugar, wait." Marie grabbed her gently by the arm, stopping her. "Dave, I don't see the harm in her knowing I'm pregnant again. Besides, if she's standing right here, she can't help but hear what we say."

Sugar stood very still, trying not to hear Dave's answer.

78

"'That may be, but she's gettin' the habit of listening to people's talk and I'm gonna break her out of that."

"Please, Dave. Let's not fight about our children."

"I'm not talking about 'our' children." He stomped into the kitchen. Marie let her daughter's arm go with a jerk, then whispered,

"Sugar, go on to bed. I'll be up later to say goodnight."

Sugar tiptoed up to her room, undressed and got into bed. From the kitchen, the voices, sometimes loud, sometimes muffled, seemed to repeat her name. After a long while, she fell asleep.

Joel was three when the twins were born. Dave named them Stephen and Stephanie. Like before, he was the proud father.

"I must be a hell of a man. Now I make 'em two at a time." The two basinets were in front of the living room window. With each hand, he patted a baby.
Marie laughed.
"One at a time is enough for me, thanks."
Sugar whispered to her mother.
"Are we gonna have more babies?"

Dave's smile changed instantly to a frown. He had heard her. Now he glared, yet even in anger, would not break the wall of silence which has begun the night he argued with Marie in the kitchen. Marie reached out and cupped Sugar's face in her hands.

"Hush, child. Why don't you take Joel out for a walk?"

"Okay, Mama." She put on her sweater, then helped Joel into his jacket. Taking his hand, she pulled Joel behind her and stepped out onto the porch. Her mother closed the door slowly behind the two children, but not before Dave's voice was heard again.

"Look at her and you'd see. She's not like..."

Sugar looked down at her brother's smiling face. As they neared the edge of the porch, Joel held out his arms to her. She lifted him until their faces touched, then carried him down the steps to the pavement.

Since there were only two bedrooms, the house was crowded by the arrival of the twins. Soon Stephen and Stephanie were too big to sleep in the bassinets and their parents' room. Dave quickly solved the space problem with an idea from the Sunday paper. He always got his idea while sitting in his chair in the front room, after church. At least, that's what he said.

"It's time we moved the twins out of our room, Marie."

"I don't know where we're gonna put 'em. We already got Sugar and Joel in the other room," she answered.

"Well, there's room in there for three. Two cribs and Joel's bed. I can get a sofa-bed for down here. That'll be okay for Sugar." He waited for his wife's objection.

"But that's been Sugar's room all her life."

Sugar listened, unwilling to surrender her room, afraid to voice her opinion.

"Face it, Marie. We gotta do something. We can't move the twins or Joel down here. They're too small. She's the oldest. She'll have to learn to make do."

"I just wish there was some other way." She was weakening. Sugar tried to think about something else, but couldn't. She hoped it wouldn't happen soon.

"There just isn't any other way, Marie. You can't make this house any bigger than it is. I'll see about the sofa-bed tomorrow."

A week later, Sugar was moved to the living room, a ten year old refugee. Dave brought home an old metal wardrobe and placed it in the cellar way. Marie put all Sugar's clothes there to get them out of the room that now belonged to the other kids. The house seemed to grow smaller. Sugar had no place to hide her secret things. No place away from the rest of the family. No place but the bathroom. No one could take that away because nobody knew it was hers.

In the early days of the house, there had been an outhouse in the back, but that was gone before Sugar was born. To make space for a bathroom inside, the back bedroom had been altered. The back bedroom was Marie's room. On one side a partition was erected. A toilet, bathtub and door were installed, completing the project.

In that tiny room is the only window in the house which looks into the backyard. Sugar watched the days and seasons change from behind the bathroom curtain. Other changes began within the house.

With the growth of the family, money got scarce in the house. Sugar came to think later that lack—not love of money was the root of evil. Marie could no longer give her nickels or dimes to spend at Miss Jesse's store. Sometimes, she earned pennies going to the store for Mrs. Wise. But most of the time, she was broke.

On the last day of her childhood, Sugar was in the kitchen doing homework at the table. Her mother said,

"Go get some milk from Miss Jesse's." She handed Sugar a quarter. The milk cost twenty-four cents. "You can spend the penny."

"Thanks, Mama." Sugar rushed out of the house.

Miss Jesse's was in the next block. It was near dinnertime, so the store was empty of customers when Sugar got there. Miss Jesse stood behind a counter.

"How come I don't see you so much anymore, Sugar?"

The girl peered through the glass case at the penny candy.

"Ain't had nothin' to spend." She tried to decide between a jawbreaker and bubble gum.

"What you buyin' today?" Miss Jesse asked.

"Milk for Mama. I don't know what for me."

"I'll get the milk while you choose." The woman walked to the milk case in the back of the store. Sugar looked up as she walked away. On top of the display case, right in front, was a box full of Tasty-pies. Looking at Sugar through the little piece of cellophane on the front of each pie box, there were the most delicious-looking, flaky brown crusts she had ever seen. It seemed like one of them, a lemon pie, was calling her name. She kept watching it, until somehow that pie found its way into her pocket.

She was so nervous standing there holding that pie that she could hardly wait for Miss Jesse to come back with the milk. When the woman handed it to her, she slapped the money on the counter and ran for the door. She was putting her hand on the doorknob when,

"Sugar, come back here." She stiffened and began shaking. Her hand shook clean of that pie.

"You gave me a penny too much."

Too late. The pie hit the floor with a telltale thud.

"What's that you dropped?"

"A pie."

"But you didn't buy any pie. Sugar! You stole it! Your mother won't like that. You just wait here while I lock up. I'm going home with you. You oughta be ashamed."

Sugar waited.

Miss Jesse closed up the store, then half-walked, half-dragged her home. As they entered the front door, Sugar thought her legs would collapse. Marie came toward them.

"Something wrong, Miss Jesse?"

"Caught Sugar stealing a pie. Wanted you to know, that's all. I'll get on back to the store now."

"Thanks for telling me," Marie said. She closed the door behind Miss Jesse. She looked at Dave sitting silently in his chair, a righteous expression on his face, as if he was in church and about to testify. Marie faced Sugar.

"What made you do such a thing?"

"I don't know. I just saw that pie and wanted it. Next thing I knew, it was in my pocket."

Dave jumped up from his chair,
"Little yellow liar. I always knew you'd be trouble. Ain't no thieves in my family. Any in yours, Marie?"

"No," Marie said quietly.

"Must come from her father," said Dave triumphantly. "You look at her, it's plain she didn't take after you."

Sugar looked at Dave, at her mother and finally down at her own hands, seeing something she had never seen before. She couldn't answer their questions. She hoped they could answer hers.

"Why didn't you make me brown like you, Mama?"

82

No answer came. She left the living room and went upstairs to the bathroom. She looked out the window into the night. Her eyes searched for a way to freedom as her ancestors had once sought this house, but there was nothing to see in the dark.

When morning came, Marie no longer called her Sugar. She was just Joette. The ivy now grew across the front of the house. Knitting its way across the windows, it would soon shut out the light.

Light Through the Ivy was written while I was a student of Professor Claude Koch at La Salle College in Philadelphia. Following is a letter I received from this cherished teacher at the time.

—Suzanne Brooks

LA SALLE COLLEGE
PHILADELPHIA, PA. 1914

ENGLISH DEPARTMENT   CLAUDE F. KOCH
                                                        105 BENILDE HALL

July 2, 1975

Dear Susan,

It was a delight for me to see your story in print. This must be only the beginning. You have been writing with your heart-and this means you will have many disappointments. As Faulkner said, in effect, we are surrounded by people whose writing comes from the glands-screeching voices. So a voice as quiet and graceful as yours will have trouble being heard. You, more than most, will have to sacrifice to be an artist. The full measure of black aspiration is against it. But someone must be quiet and alone-resist community notoriety-and grow in the craft. The mirror of the soul demands it, otherwise the glass is clouded with superficialities.

Our good wished and prayers go with you, your husband, and your children in this wonderful new venture.

Please let me see what you write. I shall always be interested.

God Bless...

As ever,

Claude Koch

Other Books and CDs by Suzanne Brooks

Escape Is Not An Option, collection of poems and essays. 2003:Sacramento, CA

"Miles To Go Before I Sleep" 2003 CD, Upbeat, diverse Standards and Jazz. New arrangements—swing, bossa nova, Latin, ballads and Hawaiian style jazz.. Includes "Angel's Blues" composed by George Winston for *Canoe*—the play by Diane Yen-Mei Wong. All vocals by Suzanne Brooks with Eric Tillman, pianist/keyboards/percussion and musical director/arranger. Scheduled release December 1, 2003.

"Even Sad Memories Are Sweet" 2003 CD Jazz/R&B/Pop/Broadway Torch Songs in classy arrangements. All vocals by Suzanne Brooks with Eric Tillman, pianist/keyboards/percussion and musical director/arranger. Scheduled release December 1, 2003.

CDs Coming Soon:
New and Traditional Gospel Songs: Vocals by Suzanne Brooks with Eric Tillman, pianist/keyboards/percussion & musical director/arranger. Scheduled release December 1, 2003. Will include new compositions by Reggie Graham.

Selected Poems and Stories from Ins and Outs and *Escape Is Not An Option, Poems Out-Loud, with original music by Eric Tillman.*

* Eric Tillman, exciting, talented jazz musician/singer, composer/arranger; veteran of jazz festivals worldwide; formerly played for the Temptations, Impressions, Dells, Willie Bobo and a host of others.

**Reggie Graham, dynamic, veteran jazz musician and music ministry director, New Testament Baptist Church, Sacramento, Calfornia.